SPELLING RULES!

Second edition

Helen Pearson
and Janelle Ho

STUDENT BOOK 2

Makes Spelling stick!

Name: ______________________________

Class: ______________________________

macmillan education

CONTENTS

SLLURP

SLLURP summarises the spelling strategies that you can use to learn new words.

Say	Say the word carefully and slowly to yourself.
Listen	Listen to how each part of the word sounds in sequence.
Look	Look at the patterns of letters in the word and the shape of the word.
Understand	Understand rules, word meanings and word origins.
Remember	Remember all the similar words you can already spell and relate this knowledge to any new word.
Practise	Practise writing the word until it is firmly fixed in your long-term memory.

Scope and Sequence

This scope and sequence chart is based on the requirements of the Australian Curriculum.

Unit	Page	Skill focus					
		Vowels	Consonants	Letter patterns	Morphology	Homophones/ Confusing words	Topic words
1	6	long sounds	digraphs and blends			hole/whole	holidays
2	8				-s, -es, -ed; dropping final e		
3	10				-ed; doubling final consonant		
4	12	short y as vowel sound			-y; doubling final consonant		
5	14		medial ck				
6	16	REVISION					
7	18				-ing; dropping silent e		
8	20				-ing; doubling final consonant		
9	22		lk; silent letters: kn, wr, mb				
10	24	o-e; oa				rode/road/rowed	
11	26	ue		ew			
12	28	REVISION					
13	30				compound words; plural nouns		
14	32				adding -es to words ending in s, x, ss, sh, ch, o		
15	34				irregular plurals	deer/dear	
16	36		st, str			steel/steal	
17	38		tch			witch/which	
18	40	REVISION					
19	42	oi, ai		oy, ay			
20	44	ie, short y		ey			
21	46				adding s to words ending in y; changing y to i		
22	48			aw, oor		draw/drawer, paw/poor/pour, saw/sore, raw/roar	
23	50		spr, scr, spl, thr, shr				seasons of the year
24	52	REVISION					
25	54				contractions	his/he's, they're/their/there	
26	56				-ly; changing y to i		
27	58			er, ir	adjective suffix: adding -er		
28	60			ur, or			
29	62				er, or		occupations
30	64	REVISION					
31	66				abbreviations; suffix -day		days of the week
32	68			igh	adjective suffix: adding -est		
33	70		ld	ould		boulder/bolder	
34	72				compound words: no-, some-, any-, every-		
35	74	REVISION OF UNITS 1–34					

Note to teachers and parents

Spelling Rules!

Some students are natural spellers. But the vast majority of students need formal, systematic and sequential instruction about the way spelling works and the strategies they can use to become independent, confident spellers and spelling risk-takers.

The *Spelling Rules!* program is based on sound linguistic and pedagogical theory. It is informed by research into how students of different ages acquire and apply spelling skills, and how those skills move from the working to the long-term memory. The program closely follows the Australian English curriculum. *Australian Curriculum: English* references are provided in the Teacher Resource Books. The program consists of seven Student Books, fully supported by two Teacher Resource Books.

Each student book contains units of work, with each unit designed to be used over the course of a week. The content of each unit simultaneously develops new skills and reinforces skills from previous units. The introduction of new sounds and letter patterns is logically sequenced and takes into account both frequency of use and complexity. Where appropriate, topic words from other curriculum areas such as mathematics, science and social sciences are included. When spelling rules are introduced, only known sounds and letter patterns are used so that students focus on one skill at a time. Regular revision units enable teachers to assess student progress and reinforce key rules and patterns from previous units.

The second edition of the *Spelling Rules!* program also incorporates elements of self-assessment. A simple reflection activity allows students to assess their own progress and provides you with a starting point for discussion.

Spelling knowledge

Learning to spell involves developing different kinds of spelling knowledge:

- ☆ **Kinaesthetic knowledge** – the physical feeling when saying different sounds and words, and when writing the shapes of letters and words
- ☆ **Phonological knowledge** – how a word sounds and the patterns of sounds in words
- ☆ **Visual knowledge** – how letters and words look and the visual patterns in words
- ☆ **Morphemic knowledge** – the meaning or function of words or parts of words
- ☆ **Etymological knowledge** – the origins and history of words and the effect this has on spelling patterns.

Icons used in Student Book 2

The following icons identify the main spelling strategy that students will use to complete an activity.

Say the word. (Kinaesthetic knowledge) These activities ask students to experience how sounds feel in the mouth and jaw. Changing the positions of the jaw, lips and tongue changes the sounds we make. Encourage students to pronounce the sounds and words accurately. If they mispronounce a sound or word, they may misrepresent it in writing.

Listen to the word. (Phonological knowledge) These activities focus on discriminating between different sounds and breaking up words into syllables or individual sound segments (phonemes).

Look at the word. (Visual knowledge) These activities help students to see how the sound is represented using combinations of letters, and to associate this visual pattern with what they are hearing. Students will develop the ability to know when a word does or does not 'look right'.

Understand the word. (Morphemic and etymological knowledge) These activities focus on word meanings, word families, prefixes and suffixes, spelling rules, word origins and so on – all of which help embed spelling in the long-term memory.

Practise writing the word. (Kinaesthetic knowledge) These activities develop students' awareness of the physical movement involved in writing the word. By practising writing the word a number of times and in different contexts, the spelling becomes embedded in the long-term memory.

Rule! This icon highlights useful spelling rules. The rule is always introduced the first time students will need it to complete an activity. There is also a handy summary of important rules on page 80.

Tip! This icon tells students that a special clue or hint is provided for an activity. It may be a spelling, grammar or punctuation convention, or a definition of a useful term.

Reflection
I can do this.
I am not sure.
I need help.

Allows students to assess their progress across each unit.

Student Book 2

Units of work

Student Book 2 contains 35 weekly units of work. See the **Scope and Sequence chart** on page 3 for more information. In the second edition, each revision unit gives students an opportunity to self-assess.

Word lists

In *Student Book 2*, each unit (except Revision) has a list of ten spelling words. The core words in the lists have been chosen to support the learning focus and strategies being taught in the unit.

Spelling lists enable a spelling element to be focused on, and provide sufficient examples to consolidate the teaching point. Topic words come from other curriculum areas, such as mathematics and social sciences. In addition, homophones and words that are easily confused with each other are explained and practised.

SLLURP

Each word list begins with a reminder for students to SLLURP. SLLURP summarises the strategies that will help spelling move from students' working memory to their long-term memory. These strategies are provided on page 2, for easy reference.

Unit at a glance

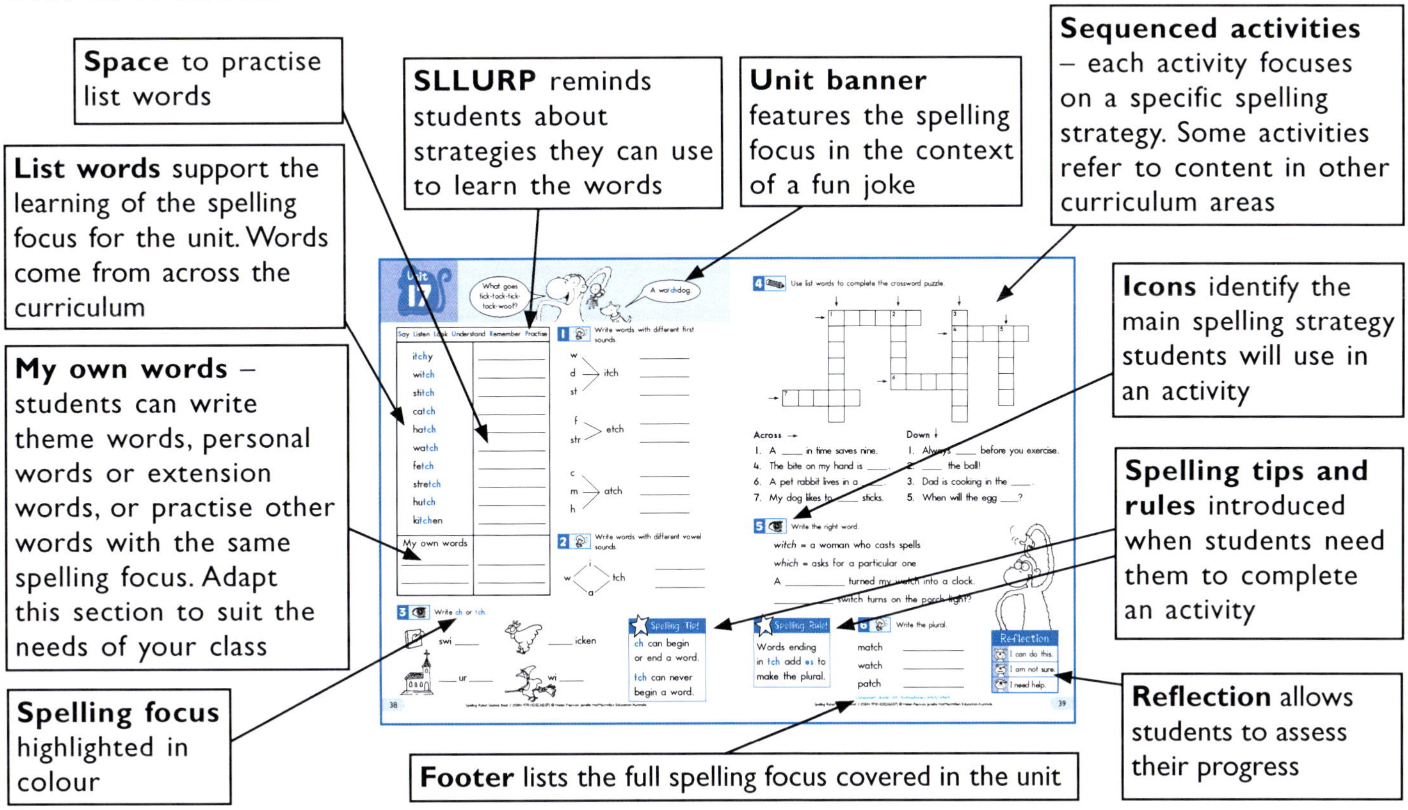

Spelling Rules! Teacher Resource Book Foundation–2

Full teacher support for *Student Book 2* is provided by *Spelling Rules! Teacher Resource Book Foundation-2*. Here you will find valuable background information about spelling development and spelling knowledge, along with practical resources, such as:

- ☆ teaching tips for every unit in *Student Book 2*
- ☆ extra word lists
- ☆ strategies for teaching spelling
- ☆ guidelines for assessment and diagnosis of errors
- ☆ activities to support struggling spellers
- ☆ worthwhile extension for more able spellers.

Unit 1

Say Listen Look Understand Remember Practise	
hole	
nice	
time	
drive	
plane	
place	
shine	
shore	
there	
holiday	
My own words	

1 Write list words in the correct tree.

2 Write the word. Then write it again, adding **e** to change the vowel sound.

3 Look for small words inside the list words. Write the small words.

place ____________ ____________ plane ____________ ____________

there ____________ ____________ ____________ ____________

4 Add a list word to make a compound word.

____________way sea____________ sun____________

5 Write two words that begin with the same sound as the picture. One of your two words should be a list word.

	list word	extra word		list word	extra word
	____________	____________		____________	____________
	____________	____________		____________	____________

6 Choose the correct homophone.

Shane ate the ____________ cake.

Jane dug a ____________ in the sand.

I tore a ____________ in my pants.

Did you see the ____________ movie?

Spelling Tip!

Homophones are words that sound the same, but are spelt differently.

hole = empty space

whole = all of something

7 Write a few sentences about your holiday.

____

____

____

____

Reflection

- I can do this.
- I am not sure.
- I need help.

Spelling Rules! Student Book 2 (ISBN 9781420236507) © Helen Pearson, Janelle Ho/Macmillan Education Australia

Unit 2

Say Listen Look Understand Remember Practise	
help	____________
stay	____________
wait	____________
rain	____________
like	____________
hope	____________
share	____________
need	____________
seem	____________
finish	____________
My own words	
____________	____________
____________	____________

1 Follow the pattern.

	add **s**	add **ed**
pull	*pulls*	*pulled*
help	____________	____________
stay	____________	____________
wait	____________	____________
rain	____________	____________
need	____________	____________
seem	____________	____________
call	____________	____________

2 Say each word aloud with **ed** added to it. Cross out the words where you cannot add **ed**.

fill	kick	bake	run
push	give	play	ask

3 A syllable makes one beat in a word. Say each word aloud. In the circle, write the number of syllables you hear.

kissed ◯	helped ◯	waited ◯	started ◯
needed ◯	asked ◯	jumped ◯	minded ◯
missed ◯	painted ◯	pulled ◯	pushed ◯

4 Choose the correct word and colour it in.

It | rains | rained | every day on our holiday.

My brother | needs | needed | a haircut every three weeks.

Spelling Rule!

Words ending in **sh** or **ch** add **es** (not just **s**).

*The hungry monkey munch**es** his banana.*
*He finish**es** it fast.*

5 Follow the pattern.

	add **es**	add **ed**		add **es**	add **ed**
push	*pushes*	*pushed*	pinch	*pinches*	*pinched*
smash	______	______	munch	______	______
finish	______	______	reach	______	______

Spelling Rule!

Words with a silent **e** drop the **e** before adding **ed**.

*The monkey smil**ed** and wav**ed** to us.*

6 Follow the pattern.

bak~~e~~ + **ed** = **baked**

hop~~e~~ + **ed** = ______________

shar~~e~~ + **ed** = ______________

cur~~e~~ + **ed** = ______________

Reflection

I can do this.

I am not sure.

I need help.

Unit 3

Say Listen Look Understand Remember Practise	
begged	________
rubbed	________
patted	________
spotted	________
planned	________
dropped	________
skipped	________
stopped	________
tripped	________
hummed	________
My own words	
________	________
________	________

1 Write the five vowels in the first column. Then write words with short and long vowels to fill in the spaces.

vowels	short sound	long sound
a	mad	________
____	________	Pete
____	________	slide
____	hop	________
____	________	huge

2 Circle the pictures that have short vowel sounds.

Spelling Rule!

If a word has a short vowel sound, double the last letter before adding **ed**.

3 Write the word when **ed** is added.

pat ________ skip ________

plan ________ rub ________

drip ________ chop ________

Spelling Rules! Student Book 2 (ISBN 9781420236507) © Helen Pearson, Janelle Ho/Macmillan Education Australia

4 Write the missing letter.

beg __ ed   rub __ ed   spot __ ed   plan __ ed

pat __ ed   stop __ ed   skip __ ed   hum __ ed

5 Write the word when **ed** is added.

stop ____________   trip ____________   beg ____________

drop ____________   skip ____________   rub ____________

slip ____________   trap ____________   step ____________

6 Say each word aloud to help you choose the correct one.

We | hopped | hoped | we could go swimming after school.

Who | pined | pinned | this notice on the wall?

Our teacher | planned | planed | a trip to the zoo for next week.

Stan | taped | tapped | the box and it fell over.

7 Write a sentence for each word.

hoped ____

____

hopped ____

____

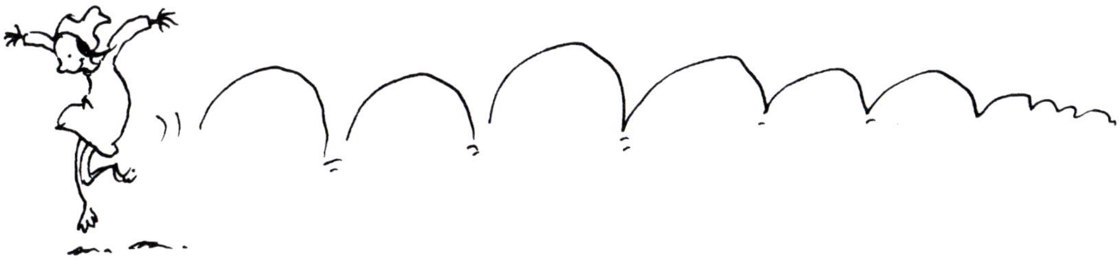

Reflection

- I can do this.
- I am not sure.
- I need help.

Spelling Rules! Student Book 2 (ISBN 9781420236507) © Helen Pearson, Janelle Ho/Macmillan Education Australia

Unit 4

Say Listen Look Understand Remember Practise	
lady	________
pony	________
sorry	________
busy	________
fairy	________
bossy	________
foggy	________
furry	________
pretty	________
ready	________
My own words	
________	________
________	________

1 Circle the word if the last vowel sound is short, like funny.

crazy cry day daisy
by busy sky pretty

Spelling Rule!

If a word has a short vowel sound, double the last letter before adding y.

fun → funny

2 Write the words when y is added.

mud ________
sun ________
fur ________
bag ________
slop ________

3 Change the first letter to make a list word. Which pairs of words do not rhyme?

(w)orry ________ (h)urry ________ (m)ossy ________

(d)airy ________ (s)oggy ________ (b)ony ________

4 Write a list word for each group. Add another word ending in a short y sound that belongs.

animals	people	feelings	weather
bunny	aunty	worry	rainy
______	______	______	______
______	______	______	______

5 Proofread this story. The story has six words that are incorrect. Circle the mistakes. Then write the correct spelling of the words in the boxes.

Tony's front tooth was wobly. When it fell out, he lost it. He was not heppy as he planned to put it under his pillow for the tooth fairy. Tony felt silly, but he decided to write a not.

> Dear Tooth Fary,
>
> I am sory I lost my tooth.
>
> Please leave a shiny coin for me.
>
> Tony

In the morning Tony rubed his eyes and felt under his pillow. He found two dollars! Wasn't he lucky?

6 Use list words to write about the picture.

____

____

____

____

Reflection

- I can do this.
- I am not sure.
- I need help.

Unit 5

Say Listen Look Understand Remember Practise	
chicken	
bucket	
ticket	
packet	
pocket	
jacket	
cricket	
kicked	
pecked	
sucked	
My own words	

1 Add ed to these words.

lock ____________

pick ____________

click ____________

pack ____________

quack ____________

crack ____________

2 Find a list word for each shape.

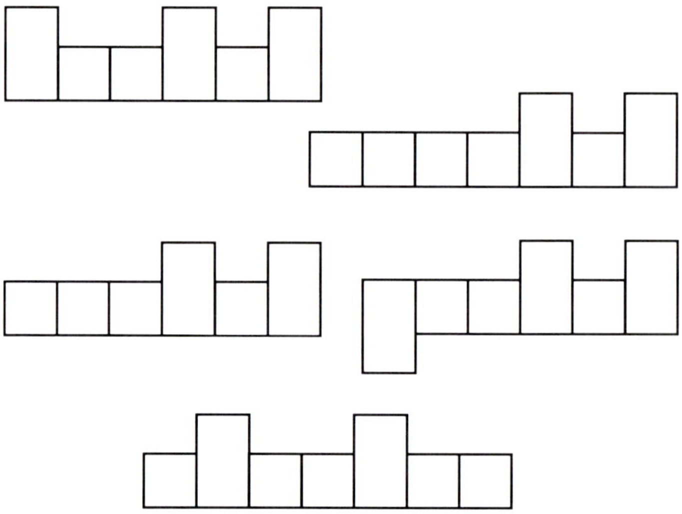

3 Write the number of syllables you hear in the circle.

sucked ◯ bucket ◯

jacket ◯ pecked ◯

checked ◯ packet ◯

4 Write a list word that rhymes.

checked ____________

rocket ____________

picked ____________

wicket ____________

5 Use the first vowel to put list words in the correct bucket.

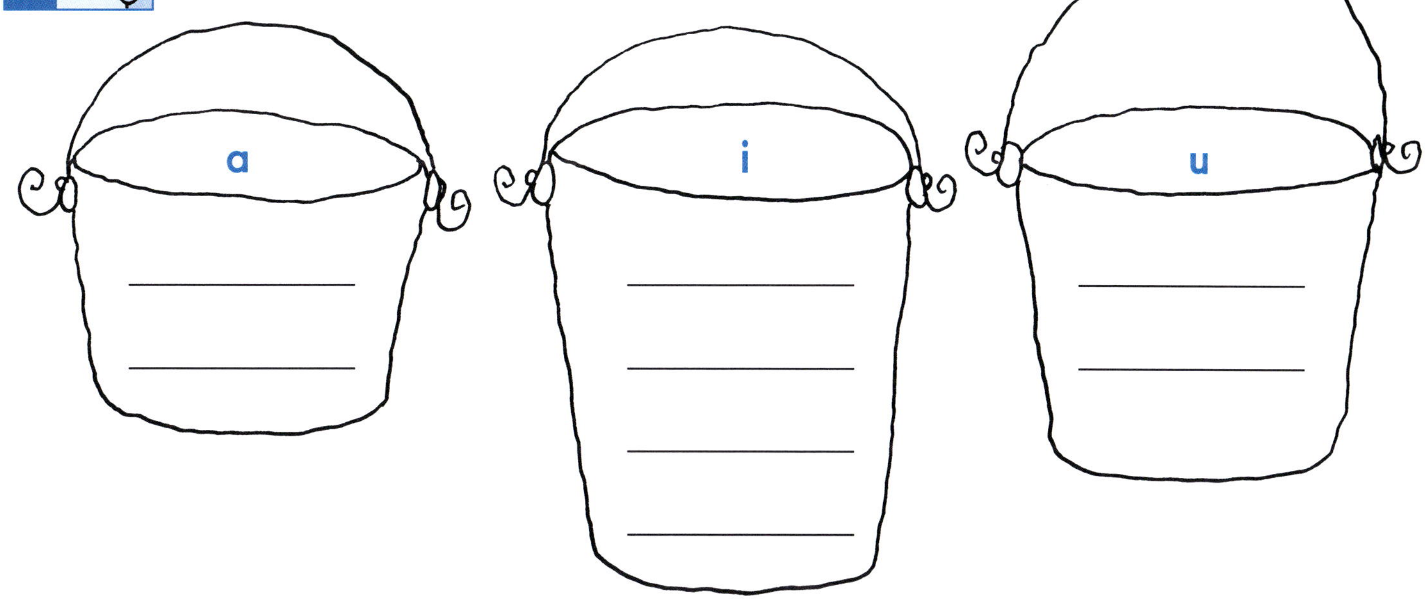

6 Change one letter at a time to make a new word. The first set is done for you.

jacket	packed	locked	packet
packet	______	______	______
pocket	______	______	______
docket	socket	ticket	kicked

7 What happened on the farm today? Choose a different word to finish each sentence.

quacked	kicked	pecked	licked	sucked	shocked

The piglet ______________ milk from its mother. The cat ______________ its paws. The ducks ______________. The chickens ______________ the corn. The cow ______________ the poor farmer! She was ______________.

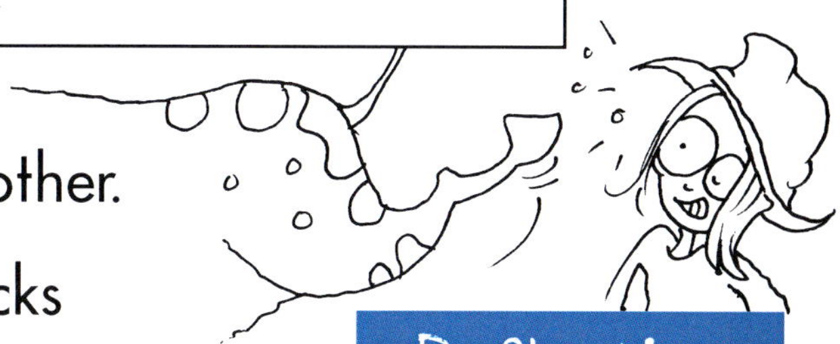

Reflection

- I can do this.
- I am not sure.
- I need help.

Consonant digraph ck in medial position

Unit 6 Revision

1 Write all the words you can see in the word worm.

____

____

2 Write the words when you add **s** or **es** and **ed**.

	add s	add ed
ask		
pat		
like		

	add s or es	add ed
wash		
share		
drop		

3 Say each word. Write in the circle the number of syllables you hear.

kicked ○ happy ○ place ○ begged ○ needed ○

finished ○ pocket ○ drive ○ windy ○

4 Draw lines to match words with the same vowel sounds.

plane ticket spotty drive shine

cricket lady time rain bossy

Spelling Rules! Student Book 2 (ISBN 9781420236507) © Helen Pearson, Janelle Ho/Macmillan Education Australia

5 Write the plurals.

three

______

two

______

four

______

6 Look for a small word inside each word. Write the small word.

seem	______	ready	______
packet	______	finished	______
fairy	______	busy	______
holiday	______	carry	______

7 What happened on the farm today? Fill in the missing letters. Then write two sentences of your own to say what else happened.

It was noisy on the farm:
the dog _ arked,
the cow m _ _ ed,
the ducks qua _ _ ed
and I rode a pon _ and
humm _ d to myself.

______

______

______

______

8 Proofread each sentence. Each sentence has one word that is incorrect. Circle the mistake. Then write the correct spelling of the word in the box.

Zac droped his bus ticket on the muddy path. [ ]

Kim packed the cricket kit and is reddy to go. [ ]

Spelling Rules! Student Book 2 (ISBN 9781420236507) © Helen Pearson, Janelle Ho/Macmillan Education Australia

Unit 7

Say Listen Look Understand Remember Practise	
going	______
doing	______
eating	______
pushing	______
reading	______
riding	______
coming	______
making	______
writing	______
singing	______
My own words	
______	______
______	______

1 Write the word when you add **ing**.

go → ______

ask → ______

look → ______

push → ______

sing → ______

Spelling Rule!

Words with a silent **e** drop the **e** before adding **ing**.

care → caring

share → sharing

come → ______

have → ______

make → ______

write → ______

2 What is Ming doing this morning?

9.00 	At 9 o'clock Ming is ______.
11.00 	At 11 o'clock he is ______.

3 Write a list word that means the opposite.

pulling ____________

going ____________

4 Write a list word that belongs.

reading and ____________

____________ and drinking

5 The same sound can be written in different ways.
Circle the word that has the same vowel sound in the first syllable.

seeing	riding / eating
cooking	pushing / doing

blowing	coming / going
playing	reading / making

6 Rearrange the words to make sentences. Don't forget to add the full stop.

holiday will We driving the to beach be this

____

making are Day on a Mother's cake We yummy

____

fell was Ling riding she when pony a

____

Reflection

I can do this.

I am not sure.

I need help.

Spelling Rules! Student Book 2 (ISBN 9781420236507) © Helen Pearson, Janelle Ho/Macmillan Education Australia

Unit 8

Say Listen Look Understand Remember Practise	
running	________
cutting	________
sitting	________
swimming	________
dropping	________
shopping	________
clapping	________
getting	________
stepping	________
beginning	________
My own words	
________	________
________	________

Spelling Rule!

When adding **ing** to a word with a short vowel followed by a single consonant, double the consonant before adding **ing**.

sit → *sitting*

1 Write the word when **ing** is added.

word	add ing
run	________
cut	________
drop	________
clap	________
get	________
step	________

2 Circle the words that follow the rule.

shake	rub	plan
spot	grow	meet
trip		chop

3 Write the missing letter.

sit __ ing

shop __ ing

swim __ ing

Spelling Rules! Student Book 2 (ISBN 9781420236507) © Helen Pearson, Janelle Ho/Macmillan Education Australia

4 Add the same double consonants to each pair of words so they rhyme.

sli ___ ___ ing	wi ___ ___ ing	ba ___ ___ ing	cho ___ ___ ing
tri ___ ___ ing	gri ___ ___ ing	cha ___ ___ ing	sto ___ ___ ing

5 Write a list word that belongs.

__________ a race

writing a __________ list

__________ still in class

6 Group the words using the rules for adding **ing**.

stopping doing singing digging writing
sleeping driving dripping hiding

just add ing	drop silent e + add ing	Double consonant + add ing
__________	__________	__________
__________	__________	__________
__________	__________	__________

7 Write about swimm**ing**.

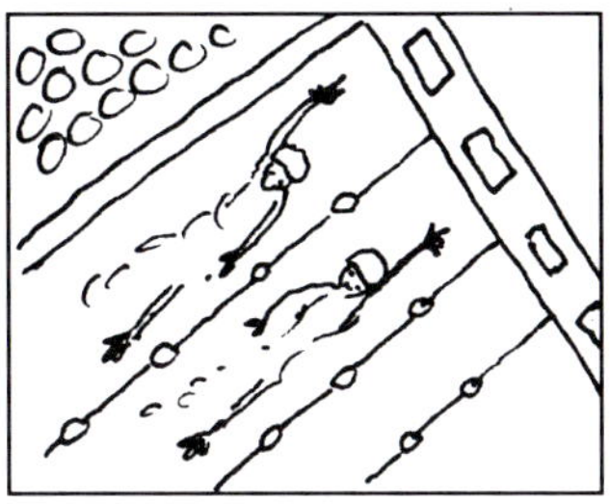

____

____

____

____

Reflection

I can do this.

I am not sure.

I need help.

Unit 9

Say Listen Look Understand Remember Practise	
chalk	______
stalk	______
knee	______
knife	______
lamb	______
thumb	______
wrong	______
wrist	______
listen	______
castle	______
My own words	
______	______
______	______

1 Write the word to match the picture.

w	alk
st	
ch	
t	

______ 

______ 

______ 

______ 

2 Circle the pictures that have the same vowel sound as **chalk**.

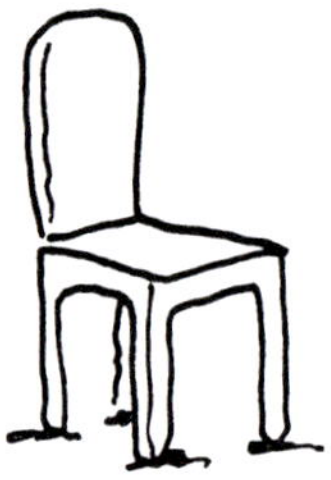  

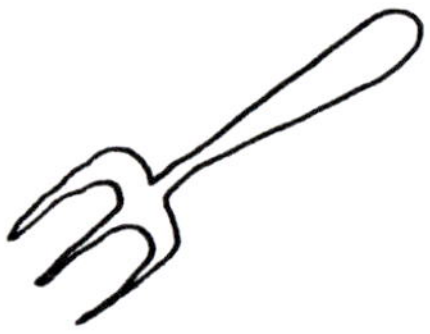 

3 Say the words and look at the spelling. Circle the silent letters.

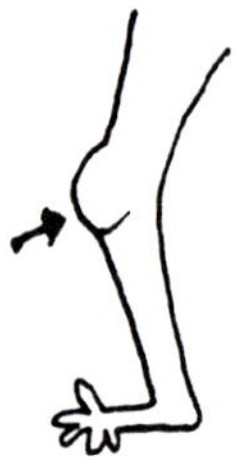
knee

lamb

wrist

listen

knot

Spelling Rules! Student Book 2 (ISBN 9781420236507) © Helen Pearson, Janelle Ho/Macmillan Education Australia

4 Write list words with the same silent letter.

write	kneel	numb	often
________	________	________	________
________	________	________	________

5 Silent letters are usually part of a letter pattern. Make words with a silent letter.

kn	ife	________	wr	ong	________	thu	mb	________
kn	ot	________	wr	ist	________	co	mb	________
kn	ock	________	wr	eck	________	cru	mb	________

6 Write all the words you can see in the word worm.

two-letter words	three-letter words	four-letter words	five-letter words

7 Add a silent letter in each space.

We __nelt to lis__en to the lam__ softly bleating.

The __nob on the cas__le door was the __rong size.

Reflection

- I can do this.
- I am not sure.
- I need help.

Unit 10

Say Listen Look Understand Remember Practise	
joke	___
bone	___
boat	___
coat	___
goat	___
road	___
loaf	___
soap	___
float	___
toast	___
My own words	
___	___
___	___

1 Circle the pictures with a **long o** sound.

2 Write a list word to match the picture.

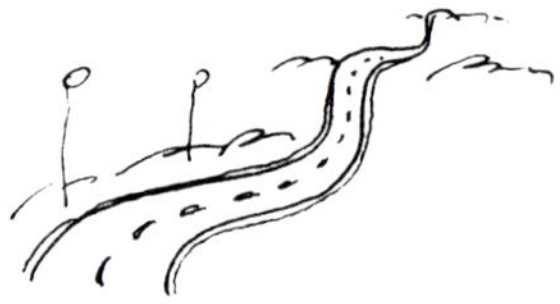

___

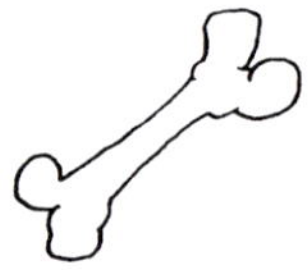

___

___

___

3 Write **oa** words.

loa — d ___
loa — f ___
loa — n ___

c — oast ___
r — oast ___
b — oast ___

Spelling Rules! Student Book 2 (ISBN 9781420236507) © Helen Pearson, Janelle Ho/Macmillan Education Australia

4 Use the clues to complete the puzzle.

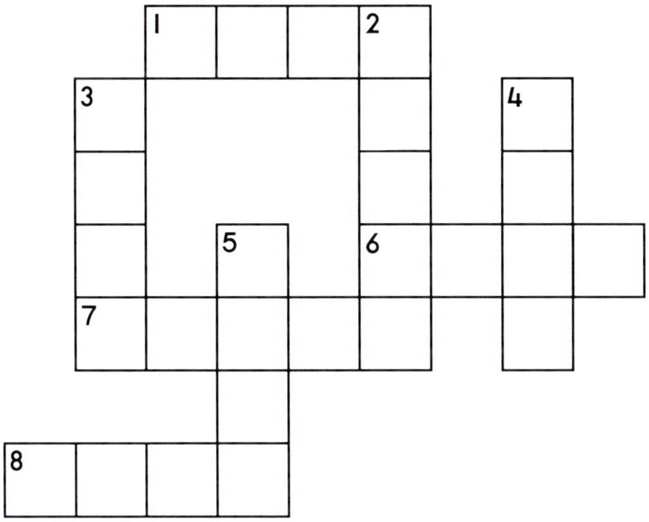

1. Row, row, row your ______ .
2. cheese on ______
3. a ______ of bread
4. wear this to keep warm
5. something funny
6. wash your hands with ______
7. lie on water
8. dogs like to chew one

5 Write the last letter to match the clue.

bigger than a frog	toa _
like a cape	cloa _
a young horse	foa _
sound of a frog	croa _

6 Add **ed** to the words.

word	add **ed**
soak	______
float	______
toast	______
joke	______

7 Colour the correct homophone.

Joan | road | rode | rowed | a pony and I | road | rode | rowed | a boat.

Why did the chicken cross the | road | rode | rowed |?

Reflection

- I can do this.
- I am not sure.
- I need help.

Unit 11

Say Listen Look Understand Remember Practise	
new	________
few	________
chew	________
grew	________
blew	________
blue	________
true	________
glue	________
threw	________
knew	________
My own words	
________	________
________	________

1 Write the words with different first sounds.

fl, ch, gr, kn → ew

____
____
____
____

bl, tr, gl, cl → ue

____
____
____
____

2 Write new words.

few	glue	grew
~~f~~ → n	~~g~~ → b	~~g~~ → th
________	________	________

3 Say these words aloud. Cross out the words that do not have the same vowel sound as the list words.

moon book shoe toe four you

4 Add the first or last letters to make all the words rhyme with **zoo**.

tw __ yo __ sho __ __ ew __ lue

Spelling Rules! Student Book 2 (ISBN 9781420236507) © Helen Pearson, Janelle Ho/Macmillan Education Australia

5 Choose the best word for each sentence.

The bird [flow | flew] in the window.

She [drew | draw] a picture and then [throw | threw] it on the floor.

When your feet [grow | grew] it's time for new shoes.

6 Add **ed** to a list word to finish each sentence.

Oh no! My dog has __________ a hole in Mum's slipper.

Have you __________ the worksheet into your book?

7 There are two pairs of homophones in the spelling list. Write them down.

Pair 1: __________ Pair 2: __________

__________ __________

Now use each homophone once to complete the story.

It was Angela's birthday. She wore a __________ dress. There were seven __________ candles on her cake. She __________ them out as everyone sang "Happy Birthday!" She __________ that all the presents on the table were for her.

8 Write the list word with the opposite meaning.

many __________ old __________

false __________

Reflection

- I can do this.
- I am not sure.
- I need help.

Spelling Rules! Student Book 2 (ISBN 9781420236507) © Helen Pearson, Janelle Ho/Macmillan Education Australia

Unit 12 Revision

1 Sort the words into groups by the number of syllables. Write a label for each group.

pocket knife grew pony beginning help reading

Spelling Tip!

A **noun** names a person, place or thing.
A **verb** names an action or what you can do.
Sometimes a word can be a noun and a verb.

2 Sort the words into three groups.

blew fairy get listen glue wrist car

Noun only	Noun or verb	Verb only

3 Write the verbs when **ed** and **ing** are added.

	add ed	add ing
need		
talk		

	add ed	add ing
joke		
drop		

4 Proofread this story. The story has five words that are incorrect. Circle the mistakes. Then write the correct spelling of the words in the boxes.

At the weekend, Grandpa and I went to the swiming pool. On the way in, we bought our tickits and a drink. The day was suny but it was cool in the water because it was also windy. After a while, it began to rane so we went hom. I hope we have better luck next weekend.

5 Find a list word that fits the pattern.

The beginning is like	The end is like	The word is
drop	five	____________
jacket	smoke	____________
think	numb	____________
knife	chew	____________

6 Write other words by following the pattern in question 5.

The beginning is like	The end is like	The word is
____________	____________	____________
____________	____________	____________

Spelling Rules! Student Book 2 (ISBN 9781420236507) © Helen Pearson, Janelle Ho/Macmillan Education Australia

Unit 13

Say Listen Look Understand Remember Practise	
sunhat	______
gumboot	______
bedroom	______
shoelace	______
toenail	______
jellyfish	______
raincoat	______
hairbrush	______
newspaper	______
wheelchair	______
My own words	
______	______
______	______

1 Draw a line to join the pictures that make a compound word. Write the word.

______

______

______

______

2 Draw a line to show the two words in the compound word.

starfish	schoolbag
earring	toenail
armchair	toothbrush

3 Write compound words.

rain — hat ______
rain — bow ______
rain — drop ______

sun — shine ______
sun — rise ______
sun — set ______

4 Write the things you see in the bedroom. Draw more items that are compound words. Write these words too.

____

____

____

____

____

5 Draw a line to match the words and make compound words. Each compound word is a body part.

arm   jaw   finger   ear   rib   belly

button   pit   cage   bone   nail   lobe

6 Write the number and word to match each picture.

______________ ______________

______________ ______________

Reflection
I can do this.
I am not sure.
I need help.

Compound words; plural nouns

Unit 14

Say Listen Look Understand Remember Practise	
buses	____________
foxes	____________
classes	____________
dresses	____________
wishes	____________
brushes	____________
lunches	____________
branches	____________
potatoes	____________
tomatoes	____________
My own words	
____________	____________
____________	____________

Spelling Rule!

Add **es** to make the plural when the word ends in:

s	*buses*
x	*foxes*
ss	*dresses*
sh	*brushes*
ch	*lunches*

1 Write the plurals.

noun	plural
bus	____________
fox	____________
class	____________
wish	____________
bench	____________

2 Write the plural for these nouns.

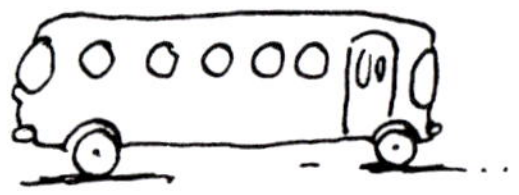

____________ ____________ ____________

____________ ____________

3 Write the plural.

sock	______________	hairbrush	______________
dress	______________	lunchbox	______________
shirt	______________	branch	______________
church	______________	text	______________

Spelling Rule! Add **es** to make the plural when **o** is the last letter and it follows a consonant.

potato → *potato***es**

4 Write the plural.

one tomato, two ______________

one volcano, two ______________

5 Use a list word to finish each sentence.

When it rains the children eat their ____________ inside.

Don't pick the ____________ until they are ripe!

I like mashed ____________ with gravy for dinner.

6 Imagine you have three wishes. Write what you would wish for.

____

____

____

____

____

Reflection

- I can do this.
- I am not sure.
- I need help.

Unit 15

Say Listen Look Understand Remember Practise	
fish	__________
deer	__________
sheep	__________
mice	__________
feet	__________
teeth	__________
geese	__________
oxen	__________
children	__________
women	__________
My own words	
__________	__________
__________	__________

Spelling Tip!

Some nouns do not change when they are plural.

1 Write the singular or plural.

one ________ two fish

one deer two ________

one sheep two ________

Spelling Tip!

Some nouns change when they are plural. *tooth* → *teeth*

2 Fill in the missing letters to show the plural word.

ox _ n m _ ce f _ _ t wom _ n child _ _ n

3 Fill in the missing letters to show the singular word.

g _ _ se m _ _ se t _ _ th f _ _ t wom _ n

4 Use a list word in each space.

Cats chase rats and __________ whenever they see them.

At the farm I saw __________, __________ and __________.

__________ pay half price for movie tickets.

5 Fill in the missing vowels.

Ther__ wer__ tw__ w__m__n, thre__ m__n and four ch__ldre__n on the b__s. H__w m__ny f__ __t are th__re? (D__n't forg__t the driv__r!)

Answer __________________

6 Draw a line to show the meaning of each homophone.

deer	a shy animal
dear	special or not cheap

7 Choose the correct homophone.

Only male __________ have antlers.

Mohan drank water because the other drinks were too __________.

__________ Mr Chan,

Mike was away yesterday because he was sick.

From Sue Lee

Reflection

- I can do this.
- I am not sure.
- I need help.

Unit 16

Say Listen Look Understand Remember Practise	
stick	____________
stale	____________
strip	____________
stray	____________
street	____________
string	____________
strong	____________
stripe	____________
steal	____________
stream	____________
My own words	
____________	____________
____________	____________

1 Circle in green the words beginning with **st**. Circle in blue the words beginning with **str**.

2 Write the list word that contains the smaller word.

ring ____________

tick ____________

ripe ____________

tray ____________

tea ____________

3 Use the vowel sounds to group the list words.

sounds like **fit**	sounds like **side**	sounds like **feel**	sounds like **make**
____________	____________	____________	____________
____________	sounds like **stop**	____________	____________
____________	____________	____________	

4 There is something wrong with the story. Write a rhyming word beginning with **st** or **str** to make sense of the story.

There is a ________ (play) dog that hangs around our ________ (feet).

Sometimes we throw a ________ (brick) for it to catch. If you don't look

after your lunch, the dog will ________ (peel) it. It likes chewing on

bones but it doesn't like ________ (pale) bread!

5 Choose the correct word.

An old | steam | stream | train is very noisy.

Dad | stuck | struck | a match to light the fire.

There's a grass | stain | strain | on the knee of my pants.

Flick out the | sting | string | if you are | sting | stung | by a bee.

6 Add two letters at a time to make a new word.

in

__ in __

__ __ __ in __

am

__ __ am

__ __ __ __ am

7 Choose the correct homophone.

steel = metal

steal = take from someone

It is wrong to ________ .

A magnet picks up ________ pins.

Reflection

I can do this.

I am not sure.

I need help.

Unit 17

Say Listen Look Understand Remember Practise	
itchy	______
witch	______
stitch	______
catch	______
hatch	______
watch	______
fetch	______
stretch	______
hutch	______
kitchen	______
My own words	
______	______
______	______

1 Write words with different first sounds.

w, d, st → itch ______ ______ ______

f, str → etch ______ ______

c, m, h → atch ______ ______ ______

2 Write words with different vowel sounds.

w + i / a + tch ______ ______

3 Write ch or tch.

swi ______

______ icken

____ ur ______

wi ______

Spelling Tip!

ch can begin or end a word.

tch can never begin a word.

Spelling Rules! Student Book 2 (ISBN 9781420236507) © Helen Pearson, Janelle Ho/Macmillan Education Australia

4 Use list words to complete the crossword puzzle.

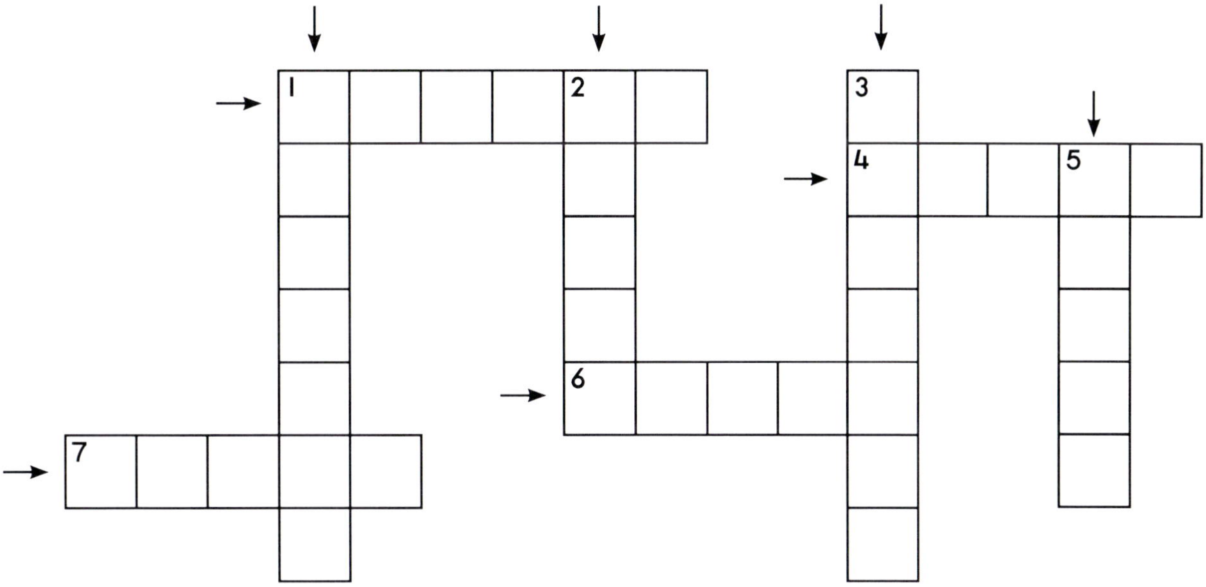

Across →

1. A ____ in time saves nine.
4. The bite on my hand is ____.
6. A pet rabbit lives in a ____.
7. My dog likes to ____ sticks.

Down ↓

1. Always ____ before you exercise.
2. ____ the ball!
3. Dad is cooking in the ____.
5. When will the egg ____?

5 Write the right word.

witch = a woman who casts spells

which = asks for a particular one

A ____________ turned my watch into a clock.

____________ switch turns on the porch light?

Spelling Rule!

Words ending in **tch** add **es** to make the plural.

6 Write the plural.

match ____________

watch ____________

patch ____________

Reflection

I can do this.

I am not sure.

I need help.

Consonant cluster tch; homophones witch/which

Unit 18 Revision

1 Choose the right plural ending. Write the word.

	add s or es
chicken	
shoelace	
class	
watch	
street	
wish	

2 Write the plural.

one coat, two ____________

one plane, two ____________

one child, two ____________

one witch, two ____________

one stripe, two ____________

one tomato, two ____________

one jellyfish, two ____________

3 If the letters show the first sound, tick the left box. If the letters show the middle sound, tick the middle box. If the letters show the last sound, tick the right box.

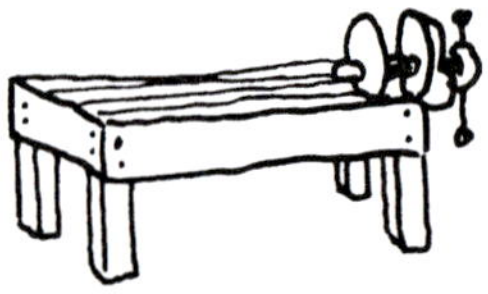
ch ☐☐☐

i ☐☐☐

th ☐☐☐

ck ☐☐☐

sh ☐☐☐

y ☐☐☐

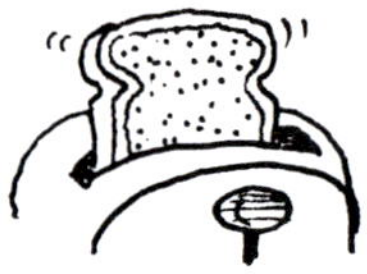
st ☐☐☐

str ☐☐☐

4 Draw a line to join up the words that have the same middle sound.

wand	thumb	grew	road	geese
hutch	stream	bone	watch	blue

Spelling Rules! Student Book 2 (ISBN 9781420236507) © Helen Pearson, Janelle Ho/Macmillan Education Australia

5 Write the past tense.

stay	*stayed*
wish	________
strip	________
like	________
chew	________
eat	________
watch	________

6 Add **ing**.

rain	*raining*
drive	________
walk	________
stop	________
run	________
wake	________
stretch	________

7 Write the words for the pictures. Circle the silent letter.

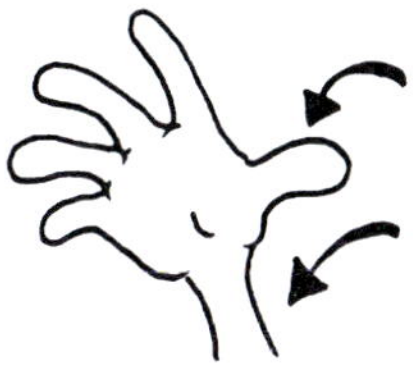

____

____

____

____

8 Proofread this story. The story has five words that are incorrect. Circle the mistakes. Then write the correct spelling of the words in the clouds.

It was raining and Tony wanted to visit his grandparents. He new his mum would not be happy if he got wet. He put on his raincote. It reached his nees. He looked for his gumboots and pulld them on. He tied his rainhat under his chin and went out to the streat. Bother! It was not raining anymore.

Revision

Unit 19

Say Listen Look Understand Remember Practise	
enjoy	________
toyshop	________
oil	________
boil	________
join	________
spoil	________
sail	________
trail	________
chain	________
fair	________
My own words	
________	________
________	________

1 Write words with different first sounds.

b, f, sp → oil
____
____
____

n, s, p, f, tr → ail
____
____
____
____
____

str, pl, ch, br → ain
____
____
____
____

2 Write words with different last sounds.

coi < l, n
____
____

rai < l, n
____
____

3 Remove one or two letters to make a smaller word.

snail	spoil	trail	enjoy	joint	fairy
________	________	________	________	________	________

Spelling Rules! Student Book 2 (ISBN 9781420236507)

Spelling Tip!

oy sounds the same as **oi**.
ay sounds the same as **ai**.
A syllable with **oi** or **ai** must always end in a consonant.

boy	*boil*	*say*	*sail*
toy	*toil*	*ray*	*rain*
joy	*join*	*way*	*wait*

4 Fill in **oy** or **oi** to show the vowel sound.

t__ __ box

t__ __let

5 Fill in **ay** or **ai** to show the vowel sound.

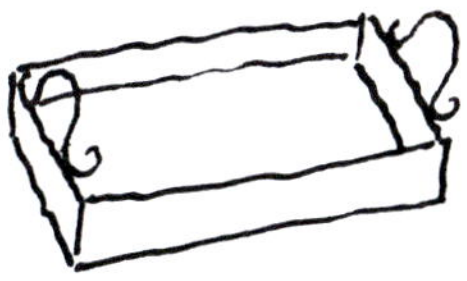

tr__ __

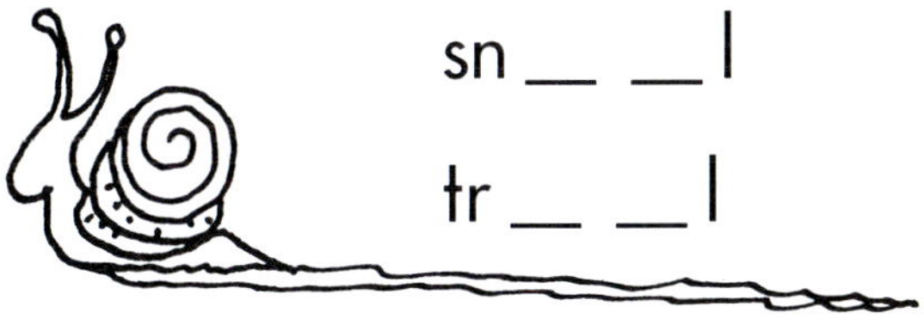

sn__ __l

tr__ __l

6 Write a list word to match each shape.

You should ☐☐☐☐☐ up your bike so it won't be stolen.

Why don't you ☐☐☐☐ in the game of cricket?

7 Write one sentence using all three words.

enjoy
sail
spoil

____

____

____

Reflection

- I can do this.
- I am not sure.
- I need help.

Unit 20

Say Listen Look Understand Remember Practise	
hurry	______
carry	______
worry	______
key	______
donkey	______
empty	______
thief	______
chief	______
field	______
shield	______
My own words	
______	______
______	______

1 Circle the picture if the word has a long **e** sound.

2 Write the missing letters.

jell _

donk _ _

sh _ _ ld

th _ _ f

turk _ _

monk _ _

3 Which **key** words finish these sentences? They are all animals.

We often eat roast ______ at Christmas.

A ______ has bigger ears than a horse.

I like to play on the ______ bars at school.

Spelling Rules! Student Book 2 (ISBN 9781420236507) © Helen Pearson, Janelle Ho/Macmillan Education Australia

4 Change the circled letter to make a list word.

thief   marry   sorry   monkey

_______ _______ _______ _______

5 Unjumble the list words.

racry   mypet   ifech   mykoen

_______ _______ _______ _______

6 Use list words to complete the crossword puzzle.

One night, a ___(1)___ stole a ___(2)___ and broke into our school. He stole the safe where the money is kept. But when he opened it, it was ___(3)___. So he left it on the football ___(4)___ behind my classroom. The police ___(5)___ found the safe and he asked two policemen to ___(6)___ it back to the station. The next day, the thief was arrested. Now the principal won't need to ___(7)___ anymore. What a relief!

Reflection

- I can do this.
- I am not sure.
- I need help.

Unit 21

Say Listen Look Understand Remember Practise	
babies	___
ladies	___
ponies	___
jellies	___
puppies	___
flies	___
cries	___
carries	___
fairies	___
hurries	___
My own words	
___	___
___	___

1 Write the plural.

one baby, two ___

one lady, two ___

one puppy, two ___

one jelly, two ___

one fairy, two ___

one pony, two ___

2 Write the correct verb.

I carry, he ___

I hurry, she ___

You cry, he ___

I fly, she ___

You worry, Jo ___

Spelling Rule!

When a word ends in a consonant followed by **y**, change **y** to **i**, then add **es**.

baby → *babies*

cry → *cries*

When a word ends in a vowel followed by **y**, add **s** only.

day → *days*

enjoy → *enjoys*

key → *keys*

Spelling Rules! Student Book 2 (ISBN 9781420236507) © Helen Pearson, Janelle Ho/Macmillan Education Australia

3 Write the base word.

__________	→	ponies	__________	→	worries
__________	→	lollies	__________	→	dries
__________	→	daisies	__________	→	carries
__________	→	turkeys	__________	→	enjoys

4 Write the plural to complete the sentences.

One fairy flies.
Two __________ fly.

One baby cries.
Two __________ cry.

Don't give a lolly to the puppy!
Don't give __________ to the __________!

A lady hurries across the street.
Two __________ hurry across the street.

There is a pony that carries children at the fair.
There are __________ that carry children at the fair.

5 Colour the correct word.

The | monkies | monkeys | like to play hide-and-seek.

The girls dressed up as | fairies | fairys | for the party.

Stay away from | bullies | bullys | in the playground.

Our class is writing | stories | storys | set in space.

Reflection

- I can do this.
- I am not sure.
- I need help.

Unit 22

Say Listen Look Understand Remember Practise

saw	________
draw	________
claw	________
straw	________
crawl	________
lawn	________
prawn	________
poor	________
door	________
floor	________
My own words ________ ________	________ ________

1 Write words with different first sounds.

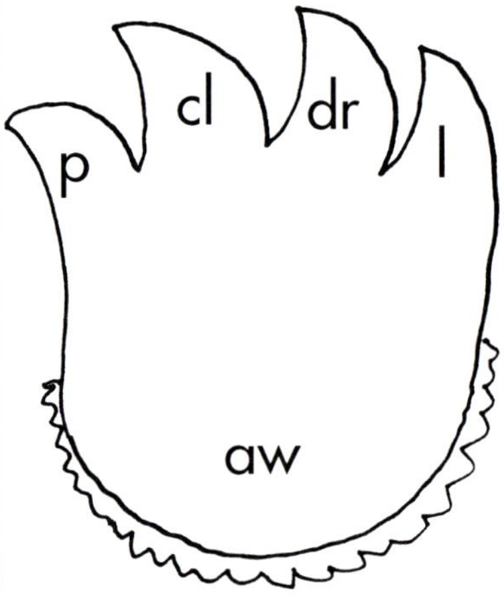

____

____

____

____

2 Circle the pictures with the same vowel sound as saw.

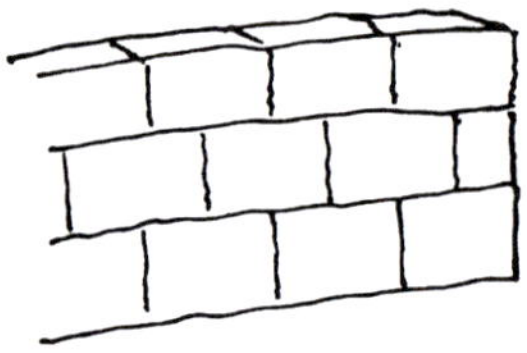

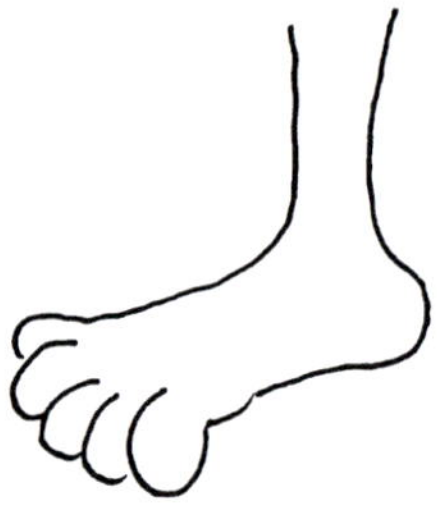

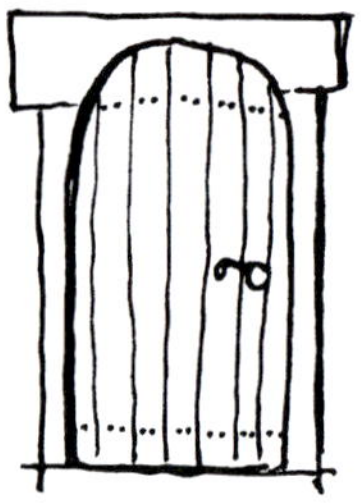

3 aw can be followed by a consonant. Write the words.

l, d, y > aw + n ________ ________ ________

cr, sh > aw + l ________ ________

Spelling Rules! Student Book 2 (ISBN 9781420236507) © Helen Pearson, Janelle Ho/Macmillan Education Australia

4 Say each word aloud. Circle the word if it makes the same vowel sound as **aw**.

join	blood	door	school	shore	roar
poor	four	more	for	floor	how

5 The same sound can be spelt in different ways.
Write a word for each letter pattern that makes the **aw** sound.

aw as in straw and yawn

oor as in door and ____________

or as in or and ____________

our as in pour and ____________

ore as in shore and ____________

oar as in oar and ____________

6 Draw a line to show the meaning for each homophone.

sore	hurting	paw	not rich
saw	looked at	poor	tip out of a jug
raw	loud sound	pour	an animal's foot
roar	not cooked	draw	sketch a picture
		drawer	place to put things

7 Colour the correct homophone.

The [paw | poor | pour] dog has hurt its [paw | poor | pour].

A dog with a [saw | sore] leg is sitting in a [draw | drawer].

Lions [raw | roar] when they smell [raw | roar] meat.

Reflection
- I can do this.
- I am not sure.
- I need help.

Digraph aw; trigraph oor; homophones draw/drawer, paw/poor/pour, saw/sore, raw/roar

Unit 23

Say Listen Look Understand Remember Practise	
spray	______________
spring	______________
scream	______________
scratch	______________
split	______________
splash	______________
throw	______________
shrink	______________
thread	______________
shrill	______________
My own words	
______________	______________
______________	______________

1 Write the missing consonants.

s __ __ ash

__ __ read

__ __ row

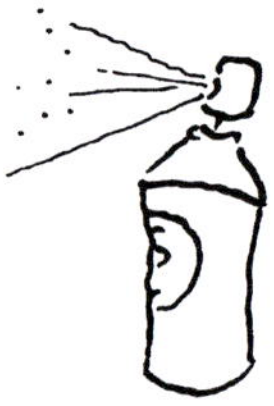

__ __ ray

s __ __ ing

s __ __ atch

__ c __ eam

s __ __ it

2 One word in each column has a different vowel sound. Circle it.

spray	spring	scream	throw
scratch	shrill	streak	how
splash	strike	thread	show
stamp	split	team	crow

Spelling Rules! Student Book 2 (ISBN 9781420236507) © Helen Pearson, Janelle Ho/Macmillan Education Australia

3 You get these words if you take letters out of list words. Write the list word.

catch sing say pit sink

4 Take letters out of each list word to make new words.

scream throw thread shrill splash

5 A year has four seasons: spring, summer, autumn and winter. Name the season in each picture. Then write one word to describe that season.

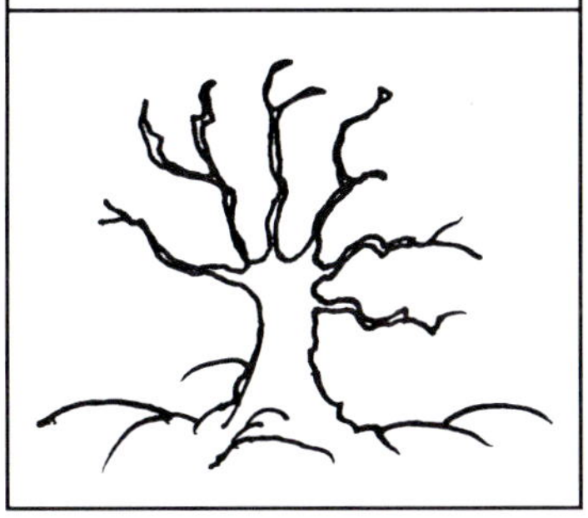

Which season has a silent letter? ____________

6 Use the beginning of the first word and the end of the second word to make a new word.

spring + hint = ____________

three + shrill = ____________

split + winter = ____________

Reflection

I can do this.

I am not sure.

I need help.

Consonant clusters spr, scr, spl, thr, shr; topic words: seasons of the year

Unit 24 Revision

1 Write the vowel sound for each word.

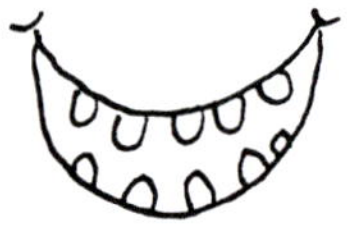
t __ __ th

r __ __ n

r __ __ d

p __ __ r

sh __ __ ld

b __ __ l

pr __ __ n

d __ __ r

2 Each of these words is a homophone.

Write another word with the same sound but different spelling.

saw	hole	paw	new	roar
________	________	________	________	________

3 Follow the pattern.

carry is to carries as worry is to ________

wish is to wishes as splash is to ________

shine is to shining as write is to ________

blow is to blew as throw is to ________

step is to stepped as trip is to ________

chew is to chews as draw is to ________

stroke is to stroked as scrape is to ________

boil is to boiling as sail is to ________

Spelling Rules! Student Book 2 (ISBN 9781420236507) © Helen Pearson, Janelle Ho/Macmillan Education Australia

4 Write a word you have learnt that matches each clue.

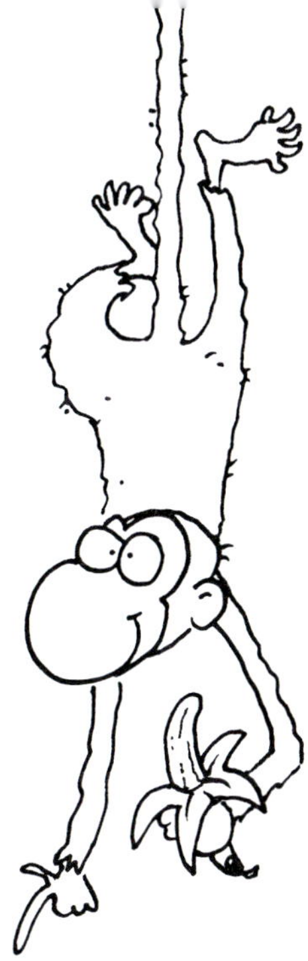

to move on hands and knees ____________

not full ____________

season between winter and summer ____________

someone who steals ____________

you need this to sew ____________

an open space with short grass ____________

5 Write a word to match each clue. Then write some clues of your own.

money + key = ____________	shrill + think = ____________
chew + thief = ____________	drink + claw = ____________
scream + match = ____________	________ + ________ = yawn
string + paw = ____________	________ + ________ = scream
sport + oil = ____________	________ + ________ = crawl

6 Describe a pet you have or would like to have. Draw a picture.

____

____

____

____

____

____

Unit 25

Say Listen Look Understand Remember Practise	
I'll	______
he's	______
it's	______
isn't	______
can't	______
don't	______
doesn't	______
didn't	______
won't	______
we're	______
My own words	
______	______
______	______

Spelling Rule!

A **contraction** is the short form of a word or words. Use an **apostrophe** to show that letters have been left out.

I will → I'll
it is → it's
do not → don't

1 Circle the words that match each short form.

I'm	I can I am I must
he's	he is he was he does
isn't	is not it is does not
can't	care not can I cannot
won't	what is will not what not

2 The window shows which letters must be taken away. Write the short word that comes out of the shrinking machine.

she is → ______
does not → ______
we are → ______

Spelling Rules! Student Book 2 (ISBN 9781420236507) © Helen Pearson, Janelle Ho/Macmillan Education Australia

3 Write list words to complete the story.

"May I please go to Alex's house, Mum?" I asked. "No, you __________," Mum said. "__________ Grandad's birthday today and we __________ want to go to his party without a present. So __________ going to the shops now and I need you to help me choose his gift."

4 **His** and **he's** are often confused. Colour the correct word in each sentence.

Ali packed | his | he's | bag before going to bed.

Don't annoy Annan while | his | he's | working.

5 **They're**, **their** and **there** are homophones. Colour the correct homophone in each sentence.

They're	Their	There	are hooks where they can hang wet raincoats.
They're	Their	There	raincoats were dry by the end of the day.
They're	Their	There	not allowed to use umbrellas.

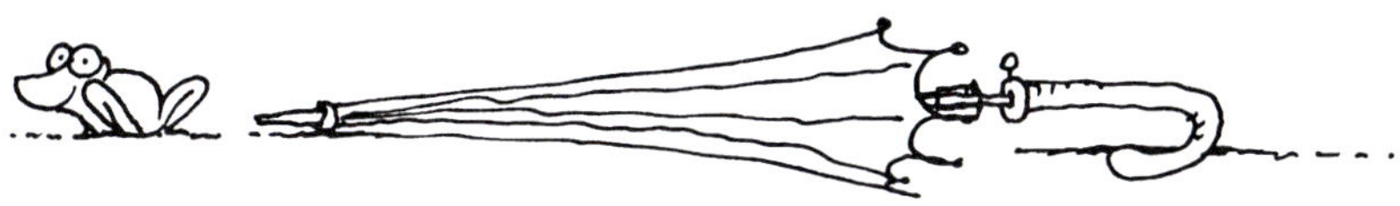

6 Write your own sentence using **it's**. Make sure it means **it is**.

____

____

____

Reflection
I can do this.
I am not sure.
I need help.

Unit 26

Say Listen Look Understand Remember Practise

sadly	______
loudly	______
slowly	______
nicely	______
rudely	______
quickly	______
quietly	______
crossly	______
kindly	______
happily	______
My own words	
______	______
______	______

Spelling Tip!

Adverbs tell us more about verbs.

Adverbs often end in **ly**.

1 Make adverbs by adding ly.

ly: proud, soft, sad, quick, strong

______

______

______

______

______

2 Add ly to these words.

nice → ______

rude → ______

safe → ______

Spelling Rule!

If the word ends with a short **y**, change **y** to **i** before you add **ly**.

If the word ends with a long **y**, just add **ly**.

3 Follow the rules to add ly.

short y	change y to i + ly
happy	

long y	add ly
shy	

Spelling Rules! Student Book 2 (ISBN 9781420236507) © Helen Pearson, Janelle Ho/Macmillan Education Australia

4 Use the sound in the base word to group the list words.

long vowel as in slowly

__________ __________ __________ __________

short vowel as in sadly

__________ __________ __________

Which word has a long and a short vowel? qu _ _ _ _ _

5 Write an adverb from the list to go with each verb.

smile	__________	whisper	__________
answer	__________	shout	__________
stroll	__________	grab	__________
run	__________	share	__________

6 Rewrite each sentence using an adverb instead of the underlined words. Don't forget the full stops.

The postman spoke to me <u>in a cross voice</u>.

____

____

I patted the dog <u>in a kind way</u>.

____

____

Reflection

- I can do this.
- I am not sure.
- I need help.

Unit 27

Why are birds always poor?

Because money doesn't grow on trees.

Say Listen Look Understand Remember Practise

her	______
fern	______
person	______
girl	______
bird	______
shirt	______
first	______
dirty	______
thirsty	______
birthday	______
My own words	
______	______
______	______

1 Circle the pictures with the same vowel sound.

2 Write **er** or **ir**. Use the list words to check.

g__ __l

f__ __n

b__ __d

f__ __st

d__ __ty

b__ __thday

3 Make as many words as you can.

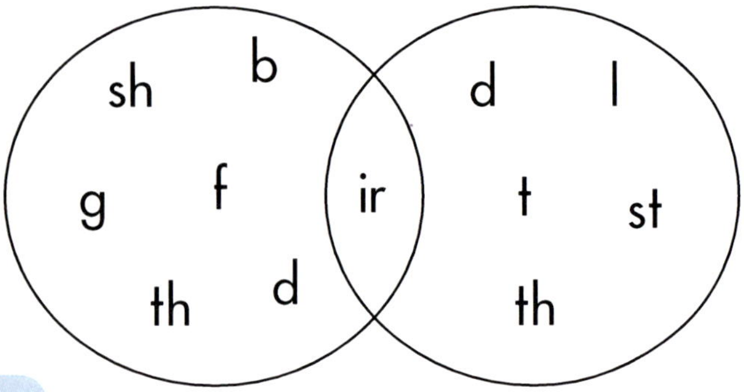

______ ______

______ ______

______ ______

______ ______

Spelling Rule!

To compare two things, add **er** to the adjective. *small → smaller*

You may need to:

- double the last consonant to keep the vowel short *hot → hotter*
- drop the silent **e** *nice → nicer*
- change **y** to **i** *happy → happier*

4 Add **er** to these adjectives.

dirty + er ______________ big + er ______________

late + er ______________ quiet + er ______________

thin + er ______________ heavy + er ______________

5 Fix these crazy sentences. Write them again, changing the underlined word.

My hands are clean, so I will wash them with soap.

____

I need a drink of water because I am so hungry.

____

Hannah came first in his running race at the fair.

____

6 Write a recount about a party at the circus.

____

____

____

____

Reflection

- I can do this.
- I am not sure.
- I need help.

Unit 28

Say Listen Look Understand Remember Practise	
burn	______
turn	______
hurt	______
nurse	______
burst	______
word	______
worm	______
work	______
curly	______
worth	______
My own words	
______	______
______	______

1 Write words with different first sounds.

b, t, ch → urn ______ ______ ______

p, n, c → urse ______ ______ ______

2 Write words with different last sounds.

wor → d ______
wor → k ______
wor → m ______
wor → th ______
wor → se ______

3 Write **ur** or **or**. Use the list words to check.

c _ _ ly

n _ _ se

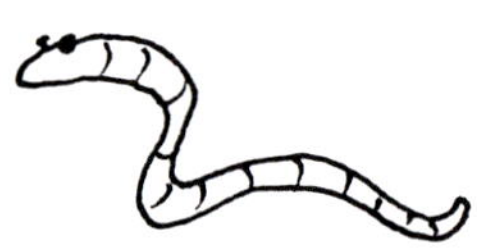

w _ _ m

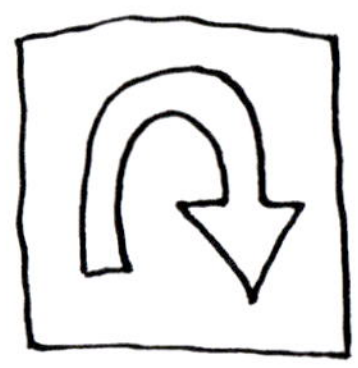

t _ _ n

w _ _ ds

Spelling Rules! Student Book 2 (ISBN 9781420236507) © Helen Pearson, Janelle Ho/Macmillan Education Australia

4 Use the clues to change Word 1 to Word 2.

Word 1	Clue	Word 2
turn	change one letter	Don't __________ the toast!
curry	change one letter	Her hair is short and __________.
fork	change one letter	Finish your __________ quickly!
curl	change two letters	Ouch! I have __________ my foot.
burn	change one letter and add one letter	Don't __________ the balloons!

5 Write **ur** or **or** words to complete the sentences.

Mrs Worthington was surprised to find a __________ in her __________.

When the balloon __________, I spilt my cup of hot chocolate. The milk burnt my knee. It __________. Mum is a __________ and luckily she wasn't at __________. She gave me some ice to put on the __________.

6 Find words in the word worm. Write them in the correct group.

words with **ur**	a word with **er**
words with ir	**a word with or**

Reflection

- I can do this.
- I am not sure.
- I need help.

Spelling Rules! Student Book 2 (ISBN 9781420236507) © Helen Pearson, Janelle Ho/Macmillan Education Australia

Unit 29

Say Listen Look Understand Remember Practise	
flow**er**	______
riv**er**	______
clev**er**	______
bak**er**	______
teach**er**	______
doct**or**	______
act**or**	______
visit**or**	______
auth**or**	______
sail**or**	______
My own words	
______	______
______	______

Spelling Tip!

er or **or** at the end of a word often names a job or an occupation.

1 Draw a line to match the word with the picture.

actor

sailor

doctor

teacher

Spelling Rule!

If a word ends in silent **e**, drop the silent **e** before adding **er**.

bake → *baker* *drive* → *driver*

If a word has a short vowel followed by one consonant, double the consonant before adding **er**.

run → *runner* *swim* → *swimmer*

Spelling Rules! Student Book 2 (ISBN 9781420236507) © Helen Pearson, Janelle Ho/Macmillan Education Australia

2 Write a list word to complete each sentence.

I work in a hospital. I am not a nurse. I am a ______________.

I bake bread and rolls. I am a ______________.

I work on a ship. I am a ______________.

I write books. I am an ______________.

I work in the theatre and on television. I am an ______________.

3 Add **er** or **or** to make names of jobs or occupations.

build ______________	inspect ______________	edit ______________
paint ______________	clean ______________	manage ______________

4 Rearrange the words to make sentences.

solving clever at Trevor puzzles is.

____

flowers yellow Mum's roses are favourite.

____

often river on Sailors the practise.

____

5 Write your own sentences using both words.

visitor
flowers

____

____

author
teacher

____

____

Reflection

- I can do this.
- I am not sure.
- I need help.

Digraph er at end of word; adding suffixes -er, -or; topic words: occupations

Unit 30 Revision

1 Make a word that rhymes.

bird	burst	dirt	turn
w_ _d	f_ _st	h_ _t	f_ _n

2 Write the contraction.

I will	________	cannot	________
it is	________	will not	________
is not	________	you are	________

3 Write the compound word for each picture.

s_ _f_ _ _ _ _ _

_ _ _ _ _ _ _ _ _ er

_ _ _ _ _ ch_ _ _

4 er or or? Write the correct ending for each word.

act_ _ farm_ _ visit_ _ driv_ _ build_ _

zookeep_ _ hairdress_ _ auth_ _ teach_ _

5 Complete each sentence.

The person who works with a doctor is a ________.

The person who works on a ship is a ________.

6 Add ly to each word.

quick → ____________ clever → ____________

nice → ____________ strong → ____________

happy → ____________ thirsty → ____________

Spelling Rule!

A **prefix** is added to the beginning of a word.

A **suffix** is added to the end of a word.

un is a prefix. **ly**, **ed**, **ing**, **s**, **es** and **er** are suffixes.

un in front of a word gives the word the opposite meaning.

un + kind → unkind *un + fair → unfair*

7 Add un to the beginning of these words.

lucky → ____________ dress → ____________

tidy → ____________ happy → ____________

8 The text has five words that are incorrect. Circle the mistakes. Then write the correct spelling of the words in the boxes.

In our class garden we grow many flowrs and ferns. We put werms into the soil and water the plants offen. The plants grow quikly. When they bloom we pick them to give bunches to our visiters.

Unit 31

Say Listen Look Understand Remember Practise	
Sunday	______
Monday	______
Tuesday	______
Wednesday	______
Thursday	______
Friday	______
Saturday	______
today	______
tomorrow	______
because	______
My own words	
______	______
______	______

1 The days of the week are often abbreviated. Write the full name for each day.

Fri. ______

Tues. ______

Mon. ______

Sat. ______

Wed. ______

2 Which days start with the same letter?

S ______ T ______

S ______ T ______

3 What day is it?

Today is ______.

Yesterday was ______.

Tomorrow is ______.

4 Look up a calendar for this year and write the day of the week for each celebration.

This year New Year's Day was on ______.

This year Anzac Day was on ______.

This year my birthday ______.

This year Christmas Day will be on ______.

Spelling Rules! Student Book 2 (ISBN 9781420236507) © Helen Pearson, Janelle Ho/Macmillan Education Australia

5 Write list words to match the shapes. Complete the sentences.

On Sunday, I ______________________________.

On ________, I ______________________________.

On ________, I ______________________________.

On ________, I ______________________________.

On ________, I ______________________________.

On ________, I ______________________________.

On ________, I ______________________________.

6 Answer the questions using **because**.

Why is today special?

____

____

Why are you looking forward to tomorrow?

____

____

____

Reflection

I can do this.

I am not sure.

I need help.

Unit 32

Say Listen Look Understand Remember Practise	
high	______
sigh	______
thigh	______
fight	______
right	______
night	______
light	______
flight	______
height	______
weight	______
My own words	
______	______
______	______

1 Write words with different first sounds.

h, s, th → igh

______

______

______

n, s, l, r, m, br, fl, t → ight

______ ______

______ ______

______ ______

______ ______

Spelling Rule!

To compare three or more things, add **est** to the adjective.

tall → tallest

2 Complete each sentence with an adjective ending in **est**. You might need to research the answers.

Mount Everest is the ______ mountain in the world.

Sirius is the ______ star in Earth's night sky.

Mercury is the ______ planet to the Sun.

Spelling Rules! Student Book 2 (ISBN 9781420236507) © Helen Pearson, Janelle Ho/Macmillan Education Australia

3 Proofread this story. The story has five words that are incorrect. Circle the mistakes. Then write the correct spelling of the words in the boxes.

Dad helped Leigh and me build a campfire at the beach last nite. We tryed many times before we got the fire started. The fire burnd britely and the flames reached highe up into the dark sky.

4 Write the name for these parts of your body.

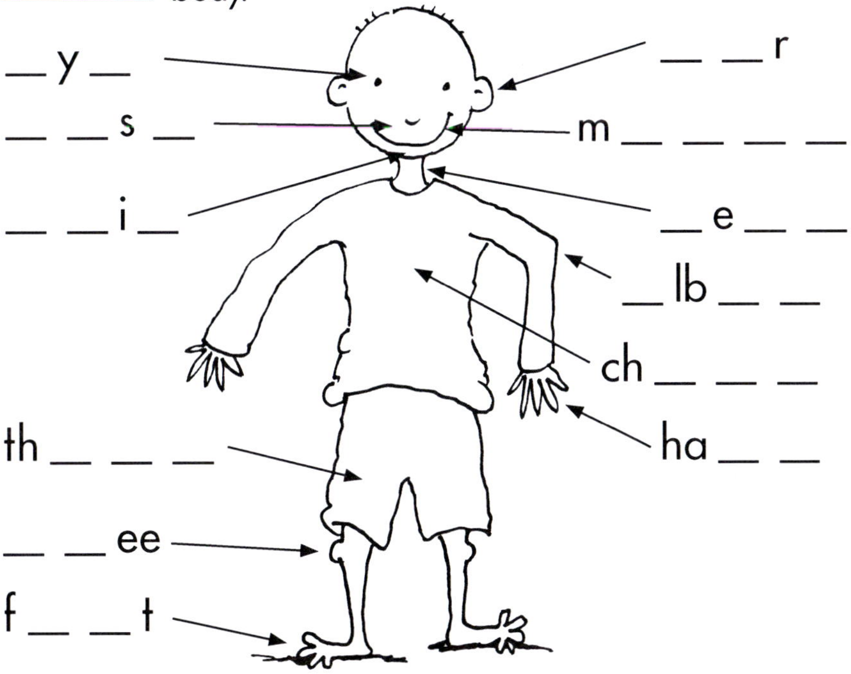

5 Do you know your height and weight?

Height:

I am __ . __ __ metres tall.

Weight:

I weigh ______ kilograms.

6 Write all the words you can see in the word worm.

____

Reflection

- I can do this.
- I am not sure.
- I need help.

Unit 33

Say Listen Look Understand Remember Practise	
build	________
world	________
scold	________
would	________
could	________
should	________
shoulder	________
wouldn't	________
mouldy	________
boulder	________
My own words	
________	________
________	________

1 Find a list word that has the same vowel sound, even though the spelling is different.

____

____

____

____

2 Write words with different first sounds. Circle the word with a different vowel sound.

c / w / sh / m → ould

____
____
____
____

3 Choose the correct word for each sentence.

would could should

Shh! The band is playing. You ________ be quiet.

Bring your raincoats, as it ________ rain later today.

Kerry ________ rather play outside than tidy her room.

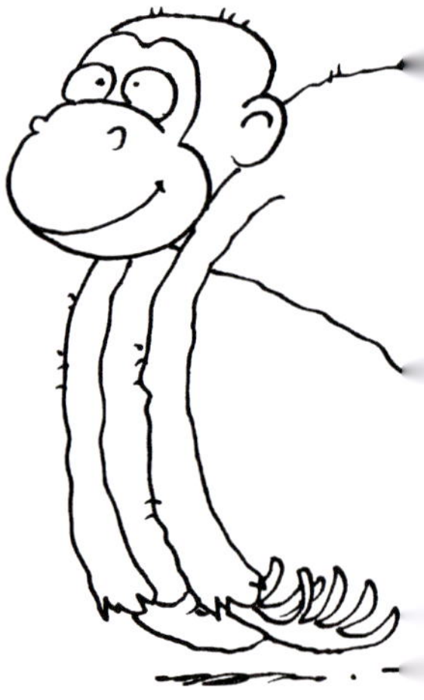

Spelling Rules! Student Book 2 (ISBN 9781420236507) © Helen Pearson, Janelle Ho/Macmillan Education Australia

4 Write the contractions for these words.

could not ____________ would not ____________

should not ____________ I would ____________

5 Add missing letters to match the meaning.

_ _ ld	not tame
_ _ _ ld	container to shape a mixture as it dries
_ _ _ ld _	covered with a fungus
_ _ ld	heavy, shiny metal
_ _ ld	with no hair
_ _ ld	past tense of "sell"
_ _ _ _ ld _ _	where your arm joins your body
_ _ _ ld	tell someone they've done something wrong

6 Choose the correct homophone.

boulder = large rock *bolder* = more bold or braver

A large [boulder | bolder] rolled down the mountain in the landslide.

I am shy. My sister is [boulder | bolder], so she chats with all our neighbours.

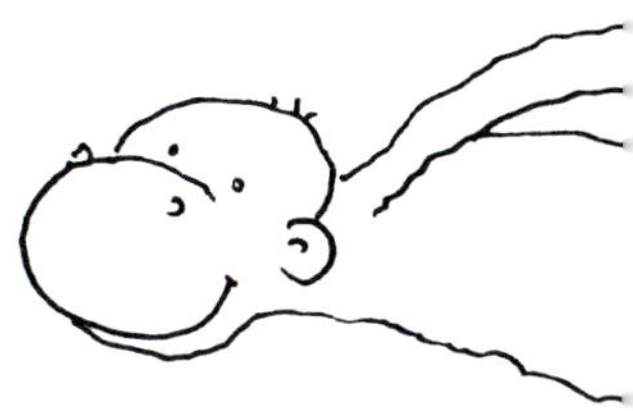

7 Write your own sentences to describe the picture.

____

____

____

____

Reflection

- I can do this.
- I am not sure.
- I need help.

Unit 34

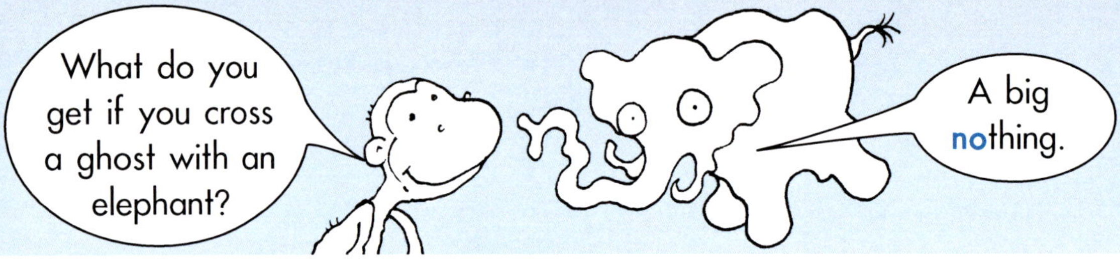

Say Listen Look Understand Remember Practise	
no one	
nothing	
nowhere	
somebody	
something	
anyone	
anything	
another	
everyone	
everywhere	
My own words	

1 Circle the word with a different first vowel sound.

nobody nothing nowhere

2 Draw a line to show the two words in each compound word.

somebody	everyone
nobody	anywhere
everywhere	nothing
anything	nowhere
somewhere	everything
anyone	sometimes
everybody	somehow

3 Make as many compound words as you can by adding another part.

some ______________________________

____

where ______________________________

____

Spelling Tip!

BEWARE!

no one = two words

I heard the doorbell ring but there is **no one** *there!*

4 Write list words.

Old Mother Hubbard's cupboard is bare.

There is ____________ at all in there!

There is ____________ at the door. I think it's the plumber.

Mum! I can't find my football.

I've looked in the backyard.

I've looked in all the bedrooms.

I've looked ____________.

This glass is cracked. May I have ____________ one?

5 Use a dictionary to help you write these words in alphabetical order.

anywhere anyone anything anybody anyhow anyway

1. ____________ 2. ____________

3. ____________ 4. ____________

5. ____________ 6. ____________

Reflection
I can do this.
I am not sure.
I need help.

Unit 35 Revision

1 Fill in the missing consonants.

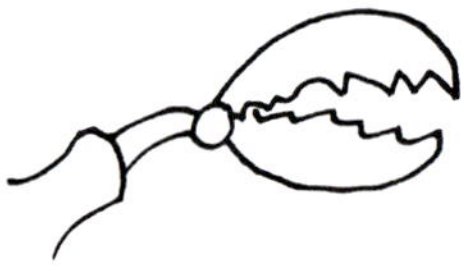

__ ea __ __ e __   __ __ a __   __ a __ __ e __

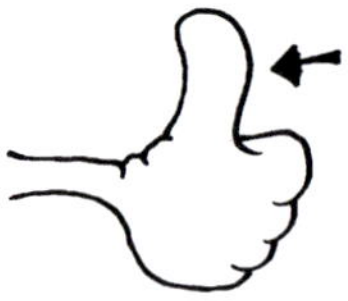

__ __ u __ __   __ __ o __ e __

2 Fill in the missing vowels.

f __ rn   gl __ __   r __ __ d   ch __ __ n   d __ ct __ r

3 Write the noun in the plural.

one joke, two ______________   one hairbrush, two ______________

one class, two ______________   one baby, two ______________

one branch, two ______________   one potato, two ______________

one child, two ______________   one sheep, two ______________

4 Change one letter at a time to make the last word.

give	grew	some	boat
__ ive	__ r __ w	__ o __ e	__________
__ i __ e	__ __ __ w	__ o __ e	__________
wire	flow	hops	been

Spelling Rules! Student Book 2 (ISBN 9781420236507) © Helen Pearson, Janelle Ho/Macmillan Education Australia

5 This is Ben's holiday timetable. What is he doing each day?

Mon.		On ____________, Ben is ____________ .
Tues.		On ____________, Ben is ____________ football.
Wed.		On ____________, Ben is ____________ .
Thurs.		On ____________, Ben is ____________ a kite.
Fri.	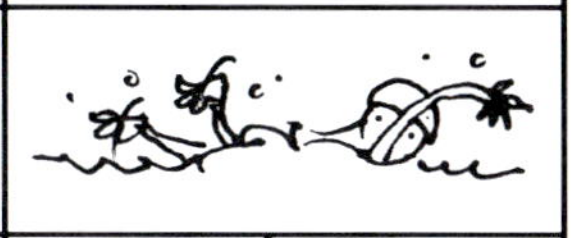	On ____________, Ben is ____________ .
Sat.		On ____________, it is ____________ .

6 Fill in the missing letters to make rhyming words.

hope	bite	term	reef
s _ _ p	l _ _ _ t	w _ _ m	th _ _ f

7 Add **ed** to each verb.

call	yell	scream	shout	whisper
________	________	________	________	________

8 Write a verb to complete each sentence.

"I am not!" ____________ Finn angrily.

"I lost my watch," ____________ Yuki softly.

"Let's go!" ____________ Gita happily.

"Have you been good?" ____________ Santa.

Unit 1
hole
nice
time
drive
plane
place
shine
shore
there
holiday

Unit 2
help
stay
wait
rain
like
hope
share
need
seem
finish

Unit 3
begged
rubbed
patted
spotted
planned
dropped
skipped
stopped
tripped
hummed

Unit 4
lady
pony
sorry
busy
fairy
bossy
foggy
furry
pretty
ready

Unit 5
chicken
bucket
ticket
packet
pocket
jacket
cricket
kicked
pecked
sucked

Unit 7
going
doing
eating
pushing
reading
riding
coming
making
writing
singing

Unit 8
running
cutting
sitting
swimming
dropping
shopping
clapping
getting
stepping
beginning

Unit 9
chalk
stalk
knee
knife
lamb
thumb
wrong
wrist
listen
castle

Unit 10
joke
bone
boat
coat
goat
road
loaf
soap
float
toast

Unit 11
new
few
chew
grew
blew
blue
true
glue
threw
knew

Unit 13
sunhat
gumboot
bedroom
shoelace
toenail
jellyfish
raincoat
hairbrush
newspaper
wheelchair

Unit 14
buses
foxes
classes
dresses
wishes
brushes
lunches
branches
potatoes
tomatoes

Unit 15
fish
deer
sheep
mice
feet
teeth
geese
oxen
children
women

Unit 16
stick
stale
strip
stray
street
string
strong
stripe
steal
stream

Unit 17
itchy
witch
stitch
catch
hatch
watch
fetch

stretch
hutch
kitchen

Unit 19
enjoy
toyshop
oil
boil
join
spoil
sail
trail
chain
fair

Unit 20
hurry
carry
worry
key
donkey
empty
thief
chief
field
shield

Unit 21
babies
ladies
ponies
jellies
puppies
flies
cries
carries
fairies
hurries

Unit 22
saw
draw
claw
straw
crawl
lawn
prawn
poor
door
floor

Unit 23
spray
spring
scream
scratch
split
splash
throw
shrink
thread
shrill

Unit 25
I'll
he's
it's
isn't
can't
don't
doesn't
didn't
won't
we're

Unit 26
sadly
loudly
slowly
nicely
rudely
quickly
quietly
crossly
kindly
happily

Unit 27
her
fern
person
girl
bird
shirt
first
dirty
thirsty
birthday

Unit 28
burn
turn
hurt
nurse
burst
word
worm
work
curly
worth

Unit 29
flower
river
clever
baker
teacher
doctor
actor
visitor
author
sailor

Unit 31
Sunday
Monday
Tuesday
Wednesday
Thursday
Friday
Saturday
today
tomorrow
because

Unit 32
high
sigh
thigh
fight
right
night
light
flight
height
weight

Unit 33
build
world
scold
would
could
should
shoulder
wouldn't
mouldy
boulder

Unit 34
no one
nothing
nowhere
somebody
something
anyone
anything
another
everyone
everywhere

LIST WORDS IN ALPHABETICAL ORDER

actor Unit 29
another Unit 34
anyone Unit 34
anything Unit 34
author Unit 29

babies Unit 21
baker Unit 29
because Unit 31
bedroom Unit 13
begged Unit 3
beginning Unit 8
bird Unit 27
birthday Unit 27
blew Unit 11
blue Unit 11
boat Unit 10
boil Unit 19
bone Unit 10
bossy Unit 4
boulder Unit 33
branches Unit 14
brushes Unit 14
bucket Unit 5
build Unit 33
burn Unit 28
burst Unit 28
buses Unit 14
busy Unit 4

can't Unit 25
carries Unit 21
carry Unit 20
castle Unit 9
catch Unit 17
chain Unit 19
chalk Unit 9
chew Unit 11
chicken Unit 5
chief Unit 20
children Unit 15
clapping Unit 8
classes Unit 14
claw Unit 22
clever Unit 29
coat Unit 10
coming Unit 7
could Unit 33
crawl Unit 22
cricket Unit 5
cries Unit 21
crossly Unit 26
curly Unit 28
cutting Unit 8

deer Unit 15
didn't Unit 25
dirty Unit 27
doctor Unit 29
doesn't Unit 25
doing Unit 7
donkey Unit 20
don't Unit 25
door Unit 22
draw Unit 22
dresses Unit 14
drive Unit 1
dropped Unit 3
dropping Unit 8

eating Unit 7
empty Unit 20
enjoy Unit 19
everyone Unit 34
everywhere Unit 34

fair Unit 19
fairies Unit 21
fairy Unit 4
feet Unit 15
fern Unit 27
fetch Unit 17
few Unit 11
field Unit 20
fight Unit 32
finish Unit 2
first Unit 27
fish Unit 15
flies Unit 21
flight Unit 32
float Unit 10
floor Unit 22
flower Unit 29
foggy Unit 4
foxes Unit 14
Friday Unit 31
furry Unit 4

geese Unit 15
getting Unit 8
girl Unit 27
glue Unit 11
goat Unit 10
going Unit 7
grew Unit 11
gumboot Unit 13

hairbrush Unit 13
happily Unit 26
hatch Unit 17
height Unit 32
help Unit 2
her Unit 27
he's Unit 25
high Unit 32
hole Unit 1
holiday Unit 1
hope Unit 2
hummed Unit 3
hurry Unit 20
hurries Unit 21
hurt Unit 28
hutch Unit 17

I'll Unit 25
isn't Unit 25
itchy Unit 17
it's Unit 25

jacket Unit 5
jellies Unit 21
jellyfish Unit 13
join Unit 19
joke Unit 10

key Unit 20
kicked Unit 5
kindly Unit 26
kitchen Unit 17
knee Unit 9
knew Unit 11
knife Unit 9

ladies Unit 21
lady Unit 4
lamb Unit 9
lawn Unit 22
light Unit 32
like Unit 2
listen Unit 9
loaf Unit 10
loudly Unit 26
lunches Unit 14

making Unit 7
mice Unit 15
Monday Unit 31
mouldy Unit 33

need Unit 2
new Unit 11
newspaper Unit 13
nice Unit 1
nicely Unit 26
night Unit 32
no one Unit 34
nothing Unit 34
nowhere Unit 34
nurse Unit 28

oil Unit 19
oxen Unit 15

packet Unit 5
patted Unit 3
pecked Unit 5
person Unit 27
place Unit 1
plane Unit 1
planned Unit 3
pocket Unit 5
ponies Unit 21
pony Unit 4
poor Unit 22
potatoes Unit 14
prawn Unit 22
pretty Unit 4
puppies Unit 21
pushing Unit 7

quickly Unit 26
quietly Unit 26

rain Unit 2
raincoat Unit 13
reading Unit 7
ready Unit 4
riding Unit 7
right Unit 32
river Unit 29
road Unit 10
rubbed Unit 3
rudely Unit 26
running Unit 8

sadly Unit 26
sail Unit 19
sailor Unit 29
Saturday Unit 31
saw Unit 22
scold Unit 33
scratch Unit 23
scream Unit 23
seem Unit 2
share Unit 2
sheep Unit 15
shield Unit 20
shine Unit 1
shirt Unit 27
shoelace Unit 13
shopping Unit 8
shore Unit 1
should Unit 33
shoulder Unit 33
shrill Unit 23
shrink Unit 23
sigh Unit 32
singing Unit 7
sitting Unit 8
skipped Unit 3
slowly Unit 26
soap Unit 10
somebody Unit 34
something Unit 34
sorry Unit 4
splash Unit 23
split Unit 23
spoil Unit 19
spotted Unit 3
spray Unit 23
spring Unit 23
stale Unit 16
stalk Unit 9
stay Unit 2
steal Unit 16
stepping Unit 8
stick Unit 16
stitch Unit 17
stopped Unit 3
straw Unit 22
stray Unit 16
stream Unit 16
street Unit 16
stretch Unit 17
string Unit 16
strip Unit 16
stripe Unit 16
strong Unit 16
sucked Unit 5
Sunday Unit 31
sunhat Unit 13
swimming Unit 8

teacher Unit 29
teeth Unit 15
there Unit 1
thief Unit 20
thigh Unit 32
thirsty Unit 27
thread Unit 23
threw Unit 11
throw Unit 23
thumb Unit 9
Thursday Unit 31
ticket Unit 5
time Unit 1
toast Unit 10
today Unit 31
toenail Unit 13
tomatoes Unit 14
tomorrow Unit 31
toyshop Unit 19
trail Unit 19
tripped Unit 3
true Unit 11
Tuesday Unit 31
turn Unit 28

visitor Unit 29

wait Unit 2
watch Unit 17
Wednesday Unit 31
weight Unit 32
we're Unit 25
wheelchair Unit 13
wishes Unit 14
witch Unit 17
women Unit 15
won't Unit 25
word Unit 28
work Unit 28
world Unit 33
worm Unit 28
worry Unit 20
worth Unit 28
would Unit 33
wouldn't Unit 33
wrist Unit 9
writing Unit 7
wrong Unit 9

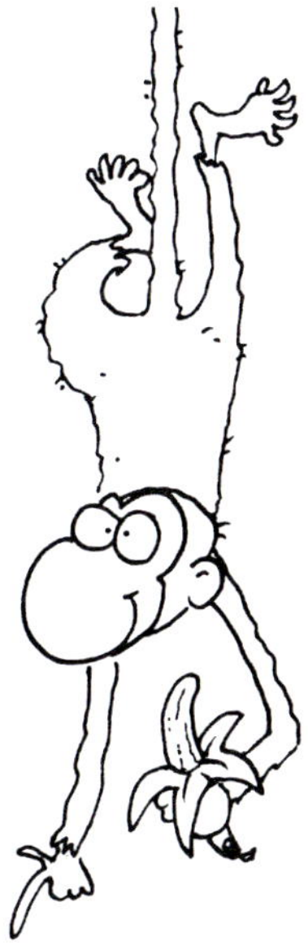

SPELLING RULES AND TIPS

To make a plural

When a word ends in **s**, **x**, **ss**, **sh** or **ch**, add **es**.

buses *foxes* *dresses* *brushes* *lunches*

When a word ends in a consonant followed by **y**, change **y** to **i**, then add **es**.

baby → *babies*

When a word ends in a vowel followed by **y**, add **s** only.

day → *days*

When a word ends in silent **e**, drop the **e** before adding **ed**, **ing** or **er**.

smile → *smiled* *care* → *caring* *bake* → *baker*

If a word has a short vowel sound, double the last letter before adding **ed**, **ing** or **er**.

pat → *patted* *slip* → *slipping* *run* → *runner*

If a word ends with a short **y**, change **y** to **i** before adding **ly**.

happy → *happily*

A word that has been shortened by leaving out some of the letters is called a **contraction**. An **apostrophe** is used to show that letters have been left out.

I will → *I'll* *it is* → *it's* *do not* → *don't*

A **prefix** is added to the beginning of a word; **un** is a prefix. A **suffix** is added to the end of a word; **ed**, **er**, **est**, **ing** and **ly** are suffixes.